MW00648654

SHE'S LIT

KARRIANNA TURNER, M.DIV.
Published by, The Girl Bible, Inc. 2017

First Printing: 2017
ISBN: 978-0-692-83887-7

All titles published by The Girl Bible, Inc., may be purchased in bulk for educational, business, fundraising or sales promotional use. For more information, please email info@thegirlbible.co

DEDICATION

To the God of the universe; the maker and creator of all things good. To the Prince of Peace, King of Kings and Lord of Lords, whose name is above every name; to Jesus Christ, The Lord of my life. I continue to be in awe and utterly amazed by your love for me. When I consider your love, my heart is overwhelmed and I am rendered speechless. I have never known love like this.

Thank you for choosing me. Thank you for looking beyond every defect, fault, frailty and deficiency and seeing me completely perfect. What kind of love is this? Thank you for forgiving and covering every mistake. Thank you for walking me through each lesson in life as my Father. When I wanted to die, it was your voice that gave me a reason to live. When I wanted to quit, you reminded me that the race is not given to the swift… When I thought that I was unworthy of anything good, you reminded me that I am the embodiment of what is good. Thank you for the journey and plans you have orchestrated just for me….. As I grow more in you, I understand more of myself. Proud to be your daughter!

5

ACKNOWLEDGMENTS

To all of the incredible people who love and inspire me every single day! Thank you for helping me to become a stronger believer and a greater woman! To my incredible **MUSE**, thank you! You keep me inspired!

To little **Miss Baylei Randolph**! Where did you come from?! You are spicy, energetic, funny, loving and beautiful! Thank you for making my heart smile with your songs when I needed them. You possess your own little light that you already share with the world! You are s STAR! And we are blessed to have you!

To MY three girls, **Carah Conner, Taylor Williams** and **GG Townsen** who keep me on my toes! I did not physically give birth to you as you each have incredible parents who are raising you to be remarkable young women! However, I am so blessed and grateful that your parents are so gracious to allow me to play a small role in your lives!

Taylor, GG and Carah, you each have been such gifts to my life! You are individually beautiful, intelligent, hysterically funny, spunky, ambitious, loving, respectful, caring and most importantly, you love and honor God. I am more excited about your future than I am my own. The Lord has blessed me to see just a small glimpse of what he is doing in your future and I am committed to exhausting myself and every resource I have to see the will of God manifested in your lives! There is nothing you can't share with me and there is nothing you could ever do to disrupt my love for you! You are stuck with me! You are each uniquely remarkable and you will contribute to the world in incredible ways! I will be watching intently, fussing, loving and encouraging you along the way! I am always here when you need me. May you go further, do more and be more than I could have ever imagined for my own life. May the light of Christ shine in you! May you be bold and fearless as you represent Him in the world! Praying God's continued favor + blessings over your journey!

Love, KARRI

ABOUT THE AUTHOR

Karri Turner, M.Div., is one of the nation's most vibrant, promising and emerging leaders. Karri is the President & Chief Executive Officer of Twenty20Something, Inc. T20S is a 501(c)3 charitable organization that provides leadership development to young women in their twenties!

Karri has received numerous awards and honors such as being named Who's Who Among American Colleges and Universities and the Distinguished Leadership and Service Award from the City of Atlanta. She was selected as a Fellow in the prestigious Front Line Leaders Academy, where she was elected as the People For the American Way Foundation, Youth Ambassador. She is an alumna of the Atlanta Women's Foundation, Destiny Fund, United Way (V.I.P.) Volunteer Involvement Program and the White House Project, New York City, Go Run Training. Karri is the former Chairwoman of the Douglas County Democratic Party and a member of Alpha Kappa Alpha Sorority. Karri Turner is at the forefront of a new generation of exceptional leaders. Karri holds a Bachelor of Arts degree in Political Science from the legendary Morris Brown College and a Master of Divinity Degree from the Candler School of Theology at Emory University. She is currently pursuing a Doctorate in Ministry with a concentration in Leadership. Karri is an author, ordained clergywoman, and motivational speaker who travels the world inspiring women.

Stay In Touch!

@mzkarribaby   @karriturner   @thekarriturner

WWW.KARRITURNER.ORG

TASTER

One of the most significant and dramatic moments in biblical history was when God, the creator of the universe, in all of his power, glory, and authority said, "Let there be light." This simple phrase was anything but simple as it served as a divine declaration and a power packed decree that would not only manifest light, but also serve as a catalyst to bring divine order into an otherwise formless, void, chaotic and dark place in desperate need of light. After physical light came into the world, we know that darkness reared it's ugly head again through the fall of Adam and Eve. Their actions brought forth and introduced a spiritual darkness into the world which created shame, condemnation, and disconnection with God. Spiritual darkness, sin, and iniquity are what mankind had become shaped in. But just as God knew what was needed at the beginning of creation to bring forth order and harmony through light, he also knew that there would need to be light sent to bring divine order and redemption to a world headed for death. This light came through the life, death, burial, and resurrection of Jesus Christ. The light of Christ is the ministry of Christ and all that it represents as it draws us out of a life of sin and judgment into salvation and relationship with God. As believers, through the transformative power of the Holy Spirit, we have been endowed with the responsibility of representing the light of Christ and sharing this light with the world.

She's Lit is a forty-day prayer and devotional journey designed to ignite the light of Christ in the modern Christian woman. "Lit" is a term used as a colloquialism which has been identified in the urban dictionary as having two primary meanings; 1). Something turned-up, popping or amazing; and 2). The state of being intoxicated. Both connotations are used in ways that can be both negative and positive.

I wanted to take this very popular term and replace the negative connotations associated with it to show that all believers are called to be lit. This light does not come from substance abuse in any way, nor is it associated with anything derogatory. However, it is sparked by the power of the Holy Spirit. Through accepting Jesus Christ in our lives, each day we are examples to the world of the redemptive power of Jesus Christ to redeem those who would otherwise be lost.

This redemption comes with the responsibility to share this light in the midst of a very dark and cold world. This is an internal light, which is fueled daily with prayer, devotion, obedience and a desire to walk in righteousness. Those who share this light, make a daily decision to choose the will of God above their own. To be a courageous living, moving, breathing example of Christ and his love for all to see!

It is my prayer, that over the next forty-days, you become reintroduced to the light of Christ! I pray that you become reinvigorated in your prayer life and intensely focused on being the best light that you can be within your sphere of influence. I pray that you are recharged, encouraged and motivated to shine your light within your homes, churches, schools, businesses and communities. I pray that every person who encounters you encounters the light of Christ and are drawn to Jesus Christ if they do not know him and if they do, I pray that they are strengthened in their walk to let their light shine brighter than ever! May every woman who has committed to taking this forty-day journey be overshadowed by the Holy Spirit! May you be blessed and fortified! Most importantly, may you be Lit!

TABLE OF CONTENTS

ARE YOU READY TO

GET *Lit*?

LET'S GO!

Day

1

" IT IS DURING OUR DARKEST MOMENTS THAT WE MUST FOCUS TO SEE THE LIGHT.

— Aristotle Onassis

Day ONE
Let there be Light!

TODAY'S SCRIPTURE:

"Then God said, "Let there be light," and there was light. And God saw the light, that it was good."
- Genesis 1:3-4 (NLT)

PRAYER OF LIGHT:

Dear Father,

"Let there be light" has to be one of the most powerful phrases uttered in the biblical text. For with these very words, you in all of your perfection, holiness and sovereignty began the process of transforming chaos into divine order. For all things that were without form began to receive clarity and definition. For you the Ancient of Day, the Beautiful One spoke and your words brought immediate manifestation as the universe instantaneously obeyed..... and there was light..... and this light was good!

Today I am reminded that when you speak, there is clarity and direction to that in which you call forth. Not only does it come forth, but it also receives your approval and affirmation. I go forth today confident in the words that you have spoken over my life. I find rest not only in what you have spoken, but the authority in which you posses that causes that word to have to obey and come forth. Thank you father for bringing forth light..... for we walk in this light in the physical world and we shine this light through our hearts in the spirit. Thank you for shaping our world with your very words.

I surrender this prayer in the name of Jesus Christ,

Amen.

#sheslit

Day

2

"

HOPE IS
BEING ABLE
TO SEE
THAT THERE
IS LIGHT
DESPITE
ALL OF THE
DARKNESS.

– Desmond Tutu

$\mathcal{D}ay$ TWO
The Light Source!

TODAY'S SCRIPTURE:
"Do everything without complaining and arguing, so that no one can criticize you. Live clean, innocent lives as children of God, shining like bright lights in a world full of crooked and perverse people."

– Philippians 2:14-15 (NLT)

PRAYER OF LIGHT:

Dear Father,

Today I ask for a humble heart and a spirit of submission as I yield to your will completely. Help me to do so willingly and with a cheerful disposition. I will not murmur or complain when carrying out the assignment for my life, for when I do so, these actions are not against man, but against you. I surrender to you and your divine wisdom, providence and plan for my life. Help me to trust you always that I will not stray from the path that you have created for me. I will endeavor to live a life that is spotless and virtuous. I will live a life that is pleasing and honorable to you as your daughter so that my life shines brightly in a world of darkness. I am aware that there are very deceitful, malicious, crooked and perverse people in the world. However, your light will not cease to shine and will prevail in darkness. Help me to be ever mindful of the world in which I live and even more aware of the God I serve and how I represent you in the earth.

I surrender this prayer in the name of Jesus Christ,

Amen.

#sheslit

Day

3

DARKNESS CANNOT DRIVE OUT DARKNESS; ONLY LIGHT CAN DO THAT. HATE CANNOT DRIVE OUT HATE; ONLY LOVE CAN DO THAT.

-Dr. Martin Luther King, Jr.

Day THREE
No Lamps!

PRAYER OF LIGHT:

Dear Father,

I am reminded that in our pursuit of you and the divine place that you have established for those who believe upon your holy and righteous name, that in the New Jerusalem, all darkness shall "cease." In this new dwelling, there is no longer a place for the night and all of the hurt, trauma, pain and dysfunction that accompanied it. Night is no longer a factor. Because of the light of your glory and majesty, I will no longer have a need or desire to seek artificial light manufactured through lamps or the sun. I am encouraged and look forward to experiencing the light that will shine directly from you. The light of my God will shine upon me and it will be more than enough to sustain me.

I seek your everlasting light today. I seek a life that is filled with righteousness. I long to be filled with your light, that I will be pleasing in your sight. Today I aspire to be a servant who serves you with a pure heart and honorable intentions. These are the servants who will be rewarded for their faithfulness with receiving your name sealed upon their foreheads and seeing your face. I pray for strength today to pursue your everlasting light. Placing your will above my own that I may reign with you forever and ever.

I surrender this prayer in the name of Jesus Christ,

Amen.

#sheslit

Day
4

THERE ARE TWO WAYS OF SPREADING LIGHT: TO BE THE CANDLE OR THE MIRROR THAT REFLECTS IT.

— *Edith Wharton*

$\mathcal{D}ay$FOUR
The Light Stops The Wicked!

PRAYER OF LIGHT:

Dear Father,

Today I am poised and rest in the assurance of the power of your divine light in the midst of a dark and cold world. I am not in fear, nor am I overtaken by the darkness of the world. I am not discouraged when those who dwell in darkness seek to prevail. I consider in your word that the light drives out the darkness, and those who are wicked will be engulfed by the light. I declare that as a daughter of the Most High God, that I will use the light of Christ within me to disturb all works of evil and malice. For where wickedness rises up in dark places to promote violence, the light prevents their works from prospering.

I yield to the light of Christ and as this light shines through me, I commit to using my life to shine in a way that disrupts and cancels the agenda of the wicked in the spirit realm and in the earth. Through faith in the power of the Holy Spirit, I believe that the strong arm of the wicked in pursuit of evil shall be crushed and defeated under the mighty hand of God. Therefore, I rejoice with thanksgiving that the works of darkness are defeated through the power of your light.

I surrender this prayer in the name of Jesus Christ,

Amen.

#sheslit

Day
5

AT TIMES OUR OWN
LIGHT GOES OUT
AND IS REKINDLED
BY A SPARK FROM
" ANOTHER PERSON.
EACH OF US HAS
CAUSE TO THINK WITH
DEEP GRATITUDE OF
THOSE WHO HAVE
LIGHTED THE FLAME
WITHIN US.
- *Albert Schweitzer*

Day FIVE
No Darkness In Him!

TODAY'S SCRIPTURE:

"This is the message we heard from Jesus and now declare to you: God is light, and there is no darkness in him at all."

- 1 John 1:5 (NLT)

PRAYER OF LIGHT:

Dear Father,

Today I accept the message delivered by your son Jesus that you are light, and there is absolutely no darkness in you. This is the truth about our holy God which we believe and cheerfully embrace. Knowing this, as your children, through adoption, and relationship with you, we are also called to be children of the light. It is our hearts appeal to be in fellowship with you, which causes us to yearn to walk-in the light. This yearning helps us to understand that we must reject those things that are associated with darkness.

I choose to practice truth and not a lie. For this reason I reject the works of darkness that consist of stealing, gossiping, fornicating, backbiting, sowing discord and every work of darkness. I pray for strength to come out of agreement with darkness and engage in fellowship with you.

I surrender this prayer in the name of Jesus Christ,

Amen.

#sheslit

Day

6

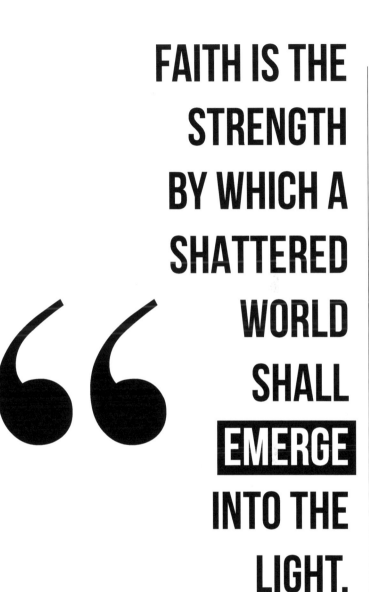

FAITH IS THE STRENGTH BY WHICH A SHATTERED WORLD SHALL **EMERGE** INTO THE LIGHT.

– Helen Keller

Day SIX
My Light & Salvation!

TODAY'S SCRIPTURE:

"The Lord is my light and my salvation - so why should I be afraid? The Lord is my fortress, protecting me from danger, so why should I tremble?"

- Psalm 27:1 (NLT)

PRAYER OF LIGHT:

Dear Father,

Today I recall the declaration of faith made by David that you God are our light and salvation. You God are the one who shines your glorious light on us that every weakness and frailty may be exposed so that every hindrance may be brought to you, that we may be strengthened through the power of your Holy Spirit to overcome every difficulty in life. You are the source of light. In you I find leadership and guidance that will turn me away from the works of darkness. I know God that in your presence is liberty and deliverance. You are my salvation, my deliverer and redeemer. For this reason, I have no reason to fear. I do not walk in anxiety or apprehension. I am not overtaken by challenges for you are with me. You are my safety and protection.

I go forth into the world boldly today, confident not in my own power and strength. However, my confidence rests in you. I will not fear anything that comes against me, for you are my father and you are in control. You have my best interest and in you I find love and safety.

I surrender this prayer in the name of Jesus Christ,

Amen.

#sheslit

Day

7

WHAT LIGHT IS TO THE EYES - WHAT AIR IS TO THE LUNGS - WHAT LOVE IS TO THE HEART, LIBERTY IS TO THE SOUL OF MAN.

- Robert Green Ingersoll

Day SEVEN
Love The Light!

TODAY'S SCRIPTURE:
"And the judgment is based on this fact: God's light came into the world, but people loved the darkness more than the light, for their actions were evil."
- John 3:19 (NLT)

PRAYER OF LIGHT:

Dear Father,

I acknowledge today that it was your son, my redeemer Jesus Christ, the light who came into the world. While without sin, he became sin that I might be saved and live in the fullness of his light. Forgive me for ignoring this fact. Instead of embracing the light, I live in a world that embraces the darkness. There are times in my life where I have preferred the darkness over your light. I have chosen to do that which is wrong instead of pursuing righteousness. I have rejected the characteristics of Jesus Christ through my thinking, speaking, actions and attitude. I know that these traits will not prevail in the presence of your holiness.

Father, I renounce sinful characteristics in my life. I am aware that those who hate sin love the light and those who love sin embrace darkness. As I pursue your holy presence, I understand that I could never live comfortably with the works of darkness, for those works are exposed by your light. Today I confess every work of darkness in my life and lay them at your feet. I recognize my own sinful nature, yet I am saved by your blood and empowered by your light. I am strengthened, forgiven and made whole in your light. I will share your light with the world through my life which has been transformed by your power.

I surrender this prayer in the name of Jesus Christ,

Amen.

#sheslit

Day

8

GIVE LIGHT, AND THE DARKNESS WILL DISAPPEAR OF ITSELF.

– Desiderius Erasmus

Day EIGHT
The Joy Of The Morning!

TODAY'S SCRIPTURE:
"For his anger lasts only a moment, but his favor lasts a lifetime! Weeping may last through the night, but joy comes with the morning."
- Psalm 30:5 (NLT)

PRAYER OF LIGHT:

Dear Father,

I am grateful today that your anger is brief. I am aware that you could very well have lasting anger towards me and all of your people. You would be justified in prolonging your anger towards me, but because of your love, your anger and frustration is momentary. Not only is your anger fleeting, but my heart is made glad by the fact that favor, kindness, grace and mercy are made available to me consistently. My soul rejoices when I consider your love and patience towards me.

Father you are intimately aware that there are dark moments in life that bring about sadness, heartache, trauma and pain which may lend to weeping. These moments in life can feel like eternity. However, I rest in your word, as I know with confidence, that the night will soon come to an end and all of the weeping and suffering I had to endure is overshadowed by the joy that is sure to come in the morning. For the morning is ushered in by the close of night and the dawning of day. When the light breaks forth, I am assured that joy will also accompany the light. Today I pray for patience as I wait in hope and expectation of the morning and the feeling of great pleasure and delight which will also come with it.

I surrender this prayer in the name of Jesus Christ,

Amen.

Day

9

WORDS WHICH DO NOT GIVE THE LIGHT OF CHRIST INCREASE THE DARKNESS.

- Mother Teresa

Day NINE
My Path Is Lit!

PRAYER OF LIGHT:

Dear Father,

I am grateful today for the power of your word. It not only nourishes my soul and satisfies my appetite, but it also lightens my way. I am grateful that through your word, I have access to light and this light illuminates my path. I no longer wonder the world confused and aimless. I do not stumble through life unclear of my direction, for clarity is found in your word.

I face the day boldly and confident that my way will be made clear and every step I take is guided by the divine light of your word. Today I remember the words of David as he expressed in Psalm 119:11, "Thy words have I hid in mine heart that I might not sin against thee." I hide your words in my heart that I may not divert from the path in which you have ordained for me to go.

I surrender this prayer in the name of Jesus Christ,

Amen.

#sheslit

Day
10

I LIVE
AND LOVE
IN GOD'S
PECULIAR
LIGHT.

-Michagelo

Day TEN
Exposed By The Light!

PRAYER OF LIGHT:

Dear Father,

I am reminded in your word today that there is nothing that is not exposed by your light. The light uncovers and makes anything in darkness transparent. As a believer, I understand that my life should be lived in stark contrast to that of darkness because I represent the light. As I live a life of light, I draw others to you. When I encounter those who do not believe, my light and example should draw them to your light. I pray that as I exercise your light in my life as your daughter, that those in darkness would see you. I believe that light duplicates itself.

Each day I rise, my goal is to walk in your light. To declare your glorious works and to share the good news of your word so that those who are asleep would arise! I pray that they would awake from darkness and spiritual death to accept your magnificent light into their lives. For if they respond to the light and invite you into their hearts you will extend your light to them and shine your light on and through them.

I surrender this prayer in the name of Jesus Christ,

Amen.

#sheslit

Day

11

"TO SECURE ONE'S FREEDOM THE CHRISTIAN MUST EXPERIENCE GOD'S LIGHT WHICH IS GOD'S TRUTH.

- Watchman Nee

Day ELEVEN
Light & Life!

TODAY'S SCRIPTURE:
"The word gave life to everything that was created and his life brought light to everyone."

- John 1:4 (NLT)

PRAYER OF LIGHT:

Dear Father,

John encourages us in the holy text that your word is the source of life. Everything created came from the word. And there was nothing that the word did not create. As a believer and follower of Jesus Christ, I receive life in the spirit. Because of this light, I have access to eternal life. I recognize that not only did I receive physical and spiritual life, but I am also granted access to the light. This light provides me with advice, guidance, direction, counsel and instruction. This light is critical to my existence as I fulfill my purpose on the earth. Your light teaches me how to live in fullness. I desire to live a life full of faith, grace and light. I can overcome fear, doubt and confusion as I travel the road of life. I rest confidently in your word and depend fully upon your light to lead the way.

I surrender this prayer in the name of Jesus Christ,

Amen.

#sheslit

Day
12

"

WE ARE INDEED THE LIGHT OF THE **WORLD**--BUT ONLY IF OUR SWITCH IS TURNED ON.

- John Hagee

Day TWELVE
Be Sober!

PRAYER OF LIGHT:

Dear Father,

As a believer who has accepted your son Jesus Christ as my Lord and Savior, I became a son of light. I understand that this is not with regard to sexuality, but through faith and adoption. I am one who belongs to the kingdom with the primary aim to walk in righteousness and morality. I am of the day and therefore, escape your judgement and indignation which is poured out on those who dwell in spiritual darkness. Today I declare that I am awake! I am watchful and I walk in sobriety according to the Holy Spirit. As I go forth today, I am alert and aware recognizing the tactics and temptations presented by the enemy.

I will remain focused and overcome all distractions. I walk in your light today and honor you in my thinking, my speaking and my actions. I will not entertain the characteristics and attributes of darkness, for I have no association with them. I hate the darkness and all that it produces. I do not sleep as those of the night, but I am alert and live in total faith, love and expectancy.

I surrender this prayer in the name of Jesus Christ,

Amen.

#sheslit

Day
13

"

IT'S NOT
NECESSARY
TO BLOW
OUT YOUR
NEIGHBOR'S
LIGHT TO
LET YOUR
OWN SHINE.

- M.R. DeHaan

Day THIRTEEN
Shine! Shine! Shine!

PRAYER OF LIGHT:

Dear Father,

I am grateful and my heart rejoices with exceeding gladness that you loved me enough to come into the world for my sake so that I would have access to the light. Because you came, I was delivered from abiding in darkness forever. There is no life or light apart from you. How can I know the way without you? How would I ever be exposed to light without you? It is impossible! I am humbled by your sacrifice of love toward me. Because you love me and have exposed me to your light, I am forever changed.

I no longer wonder in search of truth and understanding, for I have found it in you! Those who abide in darkness, abide in frustration, for they have no comprehension of truth and light. They live in ignorance, driven by their sinful nature rather than your redeeming truth. You are light and everything in darkness is an enemy to your light. I can freely walk in love, joy and happiness because of your light.

I surrender this prayer in the name of Jesus Christ,

Amen.

#sheslit

Day

14

IMPERFECTION IS THE PREREQUISITE FOR GRACE. LIGHT ONLY GETS IN THROUGH THE CRACKS.

— Philip Yancey

$\mathcal{D}ay$FOURTEEN
Embrace The Light!

PRAYER OF LIGHT:

Dear Father,

I pray for those who do not know you. I pray for those who remain in darkness with no desire to come into your miraculous light. Father I pray that you would touch their hearts and minds. That your Holy Spirit would draw them unto you. Not only that their souls would be saved and their life in eternity secured, but I also pray that you would draw them while there is still time and they can experience your light in their lives on the earth.

Draw them to you God while there is still opportunity for them to believe and accept you as their Lord. I pray that they run to you so that their minds may be illuminated and their hearts transformed. I pray that they do not walk in ignorance, but in your divine truth. Father I pray that they would be mindful of the time and accept your invitation while there is yet time. I pray that their hearts would be turned towards you that they may also become sons of light.

I surrender this prayer in the name of Jesus Christ,

Amen.

#sheslit

Day

15

THE DEVIL ABHORS LIGHT AND TRUTH BECAUSE THESE REMOVE THE GROUND OF HIS WORKING.

— Watchman Nee

Day FIFTEEN
It Is So!

TODAY'S SCRIPTURE:
"You will succeed in whatever you choose to do, and light will shine on the road ahead of you."

– Job 22:28 (NLT)

PRAYER OF LIGHT:

Dear Father,

My heart swells with gladness and my spirit rejoices at the power of your holy word. Your word tells me that I can decree a thing and that thing will be established unto me. I can develop a purpose and plan and it will not be frustrated or disappointed, but shall be established and ratified by you. I am secure that this purpose and plan will be prosperous, for it is subject to your divine sovereignty and will not be overtaken, but it will prevail!

I am grateful for your light today which you have made available to light my path and shine on my ways. I do not walk in darkness and obscurity. My path is made clear, full of light through your guidance and direction. I do not fear! I do not fret, for I am blessed with favor and success as my portion!

I surrender this prayer in the name of Jesus Christ,

Amen.

#sheslit

Day
16

IN ORDER FOR THE LIGHT TO SHINE SO BRIGHTLY, THE DARKNESS MUST BE PRESENT.

— Francis Bacon

Day SIXTEEN
Children Of Light!

PRAYER OF LIGHT:

Dear Father,

Before you saved my life, I was separated from truth, morality and any real concept of righteousness. Darkness ruled my heart, mind and spirit. I could not recognize the light of your love. Before the redemptive power of your love, I was destined for eternal darkness. My delight was in darkness and not the light. Thanks be unto you God for saving me. For you captured my heart and drew me to your love and your light. I am no longer ruled by darkness, but I walk in the brightness of your light. I share this light with the world through my union with you. As your daughter, I have access to your light because you are my father.

I share this light with the world. I pray that every person I come into contact with today will see your light in me through my actions and will seek to know my God. I am a child of light and will declare it and shine it wherever I go.

I surrender this prayer in the name of Jesus Christ,

Amen.

#sheslit

Day
17

IF YOU HAVE **KNOWLEDGE,** LET OTHERS LIGHT THEIR CANDLES AT IT.

"

- Thomas Fuller

Day SEVENTEEN
God Is The Light Everlasting!

TODAY'S SCRIPTURE:
"Your sun will never set; your moon will not go down. For the Lord will be your everlasting light. Your days of mourning will come to an end."
- Isaiah 60:20 (NLT)

PRAYER OF LIGHT:

Dear Father,

In your holy scriptures, I can rest in the prophetic words spoken for the future and glory of Zion. For you are speaking to the church helping us to know that it is through your son Jesus Christ and his light that there is light everlasting! A light that will never set or go down. For he will forever be present with his children, his saints who have overcome! This everlasting light will remain with us continually as we experience the glory.

I am thankful today that the everlasting light of your son will also be the end of mourning and sadness. There will be no more sin, suffering, trials, tribulations, heartache, distress or pain. We will be at peace in our hearts and minds. Death will be no more and darkness will be defeated. I pray that you keep my heart and mind focused on you as I strive to live a righteous life on earth that I may share in your everlasting kingdom!

I surrender this prayer in the name of Jesus Christ,

Amen.

#sheslit

Day
18

"

THE FUNDAMENTAL PRINCIPLE OF CHRISTIANITY IS TO BE WHAT GOD IS, AND HE IS LIGHT.

- John Hagee

Day EIGHTEEN
The Hidden Revealed!

TODAY'S SCRIPTURE:
"So don't make judgments about anyone ahead of time -before the Lord returns. For he will bring our darkest secrets to light and will reveal our private motives. Then God will give to each one whatever praise is due."

– 1 Corinthians 4:5 (NLT)

PRAYER OF LIGHT:

Dear Father,

You are the ultimate judge! There is none in heaven or in earth more supreme in intelligence, wisdom and in sagacity than you. It is for this reason God, I do not lean to my own understanding and I do not judge anything before time. However, I wait on you. I am imperfect and have the capacity to judge incorrectly and in error. My faculty to judge may be based upon superficial things that appear sensational and of no real value. Yet, you Lord see beyond what is made manifest on the surface to those things that are locked deep within the heart of man. You judge beyond what the eye can see and shed light on the dark and hidden things that they may be exposed.

I pray today that you examine my heart. Shine your holy light on every dark and secret thing in my heart, that it may be exposed and surrendered to you. I desire to surrender the things to you that are of darkness that I might be transformed and renewed. I am strengthened to grow in your grace. I pray that my heart is for you and that I am not self-seeking or self-serving. I will pursue a life that gives you glory. This is a life which seeks praise from you and not man.

I surrender this prayer in the name of Jesus Christ,

Amen.

#sheslit

Day

19

"

WE ARE TO
ORDER OUR
LIVES BY
THE LIGHT
OF **HIS LAW,**
NOT BY OUR
GUESSES
ABOUT HIS
PLAN.

– J.J. Packer

Day NINETEEN
Arise And Shine!

PRAYER OF LIGHT:

Dear Father,

I am aware that I am redeemed! I am reminded that I was once lost and dwelt in a place of darkness and bondage. My heart was far from you, and my way was not made known. The weight of my sin and disobedience kept me in a low and stunted state of being. But today I rejoice! For you have called me to arise! I arise out of the lowly pit of shame and despair. I am now free to stand tall with my head lifted up and my eyes fixed on you! I can shine for your light has come into my life!

Your light has redeemed me and set my captive heart free! I no longer stumble in darkness, rebellion and disobedience. My heart is for you and my desire is to fulfill your will. I recognize that your glory, honor, power, splendor and excellency is made available to me. Thank you for your love, light and glory which you have so freely given to me that I might be able to stand in your light. Today I will go forth and shine freely in a dark world! Bold, Brave and Bright!

I surrender this prayer in the name of Jesus Christ,

Amen.

#sheslit

Day
20

"LET US NOT ASK OF THE LORD DECEITFUL RICHES, NOR THE GOOD THINGS OF THIS WORLD, NOR TRANSITORY HONORS; BUT LET US ASK FOR LIGHT."

— Assorted Authors

DayTWENTY
The Illuminated Life!

PRAYER OF LIGHT:

Dear Father,

I share the sentiments of your servant Timothy, for I am not ashamed of the testimony of Christ. I will hold to it relentlessly, showing loyalty even unto suffering for the sake of the gospel. For it is through this testimony that I am saved, delivered and set free. I have been endowed with a holy calling which is not according to anything that I could be worthy of on my own accord. Nevertheless, it is according to the purpose and grace which you extended to me in Christ before time began. I recognize that this purpose is revealed to me through Jesus Christ.

The gospel was established in eternity and revealed through your son. I acknowledge that he came to earth and boldly, publicly proclaimed the good news and offered salvation. Through his death, burial and resurrection, he overcame and seized the power of death and its rule over our lives. Through Jesus Christ we receive life everlasting through the light of the the gospel.

I surrender this prayer in the name of Jesus Christ,

Amen.

#sheslit

Day
21

"I MAKE IT MY RULE, TO LAY HOLD OF LIGHT AND **EMBRACE** IT, WHEREVER I SEE IT, THOUGH HELD FORTH BY A CHILD OR AN ENEMY."

— *Jonathan Edwards*

Day TWENTY ONE
I Am The Light!

TODAY'S SCRIPTURE:
"But while I am here in the world, I am the light of the world."

— John 9:5 (NLT)

PRAYER OF LIGHT:

Dear Father,

I am grateful for the example of Jesus Christ while on the earth as he was the living manifestation of your will walking the earth. His example of love while teaching and preaching the gospel in effort to draw men unto the kingdom to be saved is the ultimate example of love and light for all people. While he was our spiritual light by which we were recovered and reclaimed from darkness, he also displayed this divine light to every person who encountered him and his ministry directly. During his time on the earth, he was about the business of the kingdom.

Today I pray God for strength, dedication and courage to model the life of Christ. I pray to be ever mindful of the precious time and opportunity that you have given me to dwell on the earth that I do not waste it, but that I use it wisely to display your light. I pray to do "greater works" that I may love, bless, heal, encourage, give, testify and perform miracles in your name so that the hearts of men would be turned towards you. I go forth boldly today as a representative of light in a world of darkness to be a living example of the power of God to save.

I surrender this prayer in the name of Jesus Christ,

Amen.

#sheslit

Day
22

"WE ARE TOLD TO LET OUR LIGHT **SHINE**, AND IF IT DOES, WE WON'T NEED TO TELL ANYBODY IT DOES. LIGHTHOUSES DON'T FIRE CANNONS TO CALL ATTENTION TO THEIR SHINING-THEY JUST SHINE."

- Dwight L. Moody

Day TWENTY TWO
The Word Of Light!

TODAY'S SCRIPTURE:

"The teaching of your word gives light, so even the simple can understand."

- Psalm 119:130 (NLT)

PRAYER OF LIGHT:

Dear Father,

I call upon you today for your leadership and guidance in my life. For without you, I know nothing and illumination is far from me. I reach out to you, for you are the all wise God, asking that my path would be lit and my way would be made clear. I open my heart to your word, for where your word enters, there shall be light. Your word gives light, which offers understanding and comprehension to those of us who are simple and humble in heart. I recognize that I need you. I thirst after your word today for it is light and life to me.

Thank you for the transforming power of your word which is alive and speaks. It loves, rebukes, corrects and discerns the intentions of my heart. Your word says in Hebrews 4:12, "For the word of God is quick and powerful and sharper than any two edged sword." I go forth today with total faith, trust and dependency on your word.

I surrender this prayer in the name of Jesus Christ,

Amen.

#sheslit

Day
23

"

IN FAITH
THERE IS
ENOUGH LIGHT
FOR THOSE
WHO WANT
TO **BELIEVE**
AND ENOUGH
SHADOWS TO
BLIND THOSE
WHO DON'T.

– Blaise Pascal

*D*ay TWENTY THREE
Light Is Better Than Darkness!

TODAY'S SCRIPTURE:

"I thought, "Wisdom is better than foolishness, just as light is better than darkness."

— Ecclesiastes 2:13 (NLT)

PRAYER OF LIGHT:

Dear Father,

This day I run after wisdom with all diligence and strength. I seek your wisdom that I may be able to rightfully discern those things that are righteous and honorable to you. I do not chase after intellect alone but that of wisdom. I dismiss folly and the foolish things of the world for they are not far reaching or sustainable. I seek wisdom over foolishness. In the same way in which light is better than darkness. For the light exposes all things, providing me with divine clarity and direction.

I will overcome the tricks of the enemy and the dangers that are ever present in darkness when the light is manifested. A fool wanders in darkness with no sense of direction. A fool yields to every trap and pit of the enemy. I pray for wisdom today that only you can give, that I may walk in the light of your love empowered by your word.

I surrender this prayer in the name of Jesus Christ,

Amen.

#sheslit

Day
24

LIGHT REVEALS RIGHTEOUSNESS, AND IT ALSO REVEALS SIN.

"

— *Theodore Epp*

Day TWENTY FOUR
Sun & Shield!

TODAY'S SCRIPTURE:
"For the Lord God is a sun and shield; The Lord will give grace and glory; no good thing will he withhold from those who walk in integrity."

— Psalm 84:11 (NLT)

PRAYER OF LIGHT:

Dear Father,

You are my source of light and you shine on me with your love, warmth, joy, gladness and peace. You are the source of light and life for all creation. It is in you that I trust. For you know what is best for me. You shower me with your love, kindness, generosity and friendship. You shine your light on me that I would not be consumed by the power of darkness. You ensure that I have more than enough. You provide me with peace as I journey on the road of life, ensuring that I will find safety and rest in you when I am faced with trials and tribulations. Your grace is made sufficient and I lack nothing.

Thank you for knowing exactly what I need and when I need it. I trust you with my life, for without you I have no life. I trust you with my destiny and the fulfillment of my purpose in your divine time. I will only pursue the things that you have divinely assigned to me. I know that if I love you with my whole heart and walk in righteousness, there is no good thing that you will keep from me. I believe that you love me. I trust today that if you have not released it to me, it is because it is not good or it is not within your divine time. I am confident that everything you have spoken over my life, shall come forth.

I surrender this prayer in the name of Jesus Christ,

Amen.

#sheslit

113

Day
25

"

GLORY IN CHRIST AND YOU CAN **BASK** IN HIS LIGHT FOREVER.

– *Woodrow Kroll*

DayTWENTY FIVE
The Glorious Light!

TODAY'S SCRIPTURE:

"Satan, who is the god of this world, has blinded the minds of those who do not believe. They are unable to see the glorious light of the good news. They don't understand this message about the glory of Christ, who is the exact likeness of God."
— 2 *Corinthians* 4:4 (NLT)

PRAYER OF LIGHT:

Dear Father,

Today I renounce Satan the god of this age and all of the influence of his works. For it is a world that lacks love and promotes hate, competition, idolatry, materialism, promiscuity, self-centeredness and everything that is counter to the kingdom. Those whose hearts are wrapped around the ideas and principles of the world have been blinded to the truth of Christ through Satan and his lies. In their unbelief they reject the truth of Jesus Christ and his ways. Father I call upon you through the power of your Holy Spirit to change the hearts of men. For you are the only who can draw them unto you.

Today I pray for women all over the world in Satan's grasp. I pray for their divine release from darkness into your marvelous light. I pray that they seek you and come into total repentance that they may be delivered from darkness and saved by Jesus Christ. We are free in our minds and can see beyond the view of the wicked one. The light of your gospel saves and sets us free!

I surrender this prayer in the name of Jesus Christ,

Amen.

#sheslit

Day
26

"

KNOWLEDGE
IS LOVE AND
LIGHT AND
VISION.

- Helen Keller

Day TWENTY SIX
Shine In Our Hearts!

TODAY'S SCRIPTURE:

"For God, who said, "Let there be light in the darkness," has made this light shine in our hearts so we could know the glory of God that is seen in the face of Jesus Christ." - 2 Corinthians 4:6 (NLT)

PRAYER OF LIGHT:

Dear Father,

In Genesis 1 it was you God who commanded light to shine out of darkness. As the ruler and creator of the universe, at your command, visible light came into existence. In this same way, you speak to my heart through the power of your holy word and your light shines in my heart and I am converted from a sinner into a child of light. I had the opportunity to have a personal encounter with your light which has snatched me from the pit of darkness. It is through the gospel, your holy word that the Holy Spirit touches my heart and shows me its condition and how my life has been entangled in sin. You show me my failures and weaknesses, and yet you beautifully make yourself available and accessible to me so that I can be strengthened, forgiven and made whole in you. There is nothing that you cannot deliver me from. There is nothing that the blood of Jesus Christ did not cover at the cross.

Thank you for the light and knowledge of your glory! For I have made a conscious decision to accept you into my heart and to share your light with the world.

I surrender this prayer in the name of Jesus Christ,

Amen.

#sheslit

Day
27

GRACE COMES INTO THE SOUL, AS THE MORNING SUN INTO THE WORLD; FIRST A DAWNING; THEN A LIGHT; AND AT LAST THE SUN IN HIS FULL AND **EXCELLENT** BRIGHTNESS.

- Thomas Adams

Day TWENTY SEVEN
Stay Alert!

PRAYER OF LIGHT:

Dear Father,

As your daughter who is of the day, who walks in the light according to your word, I pray for strength and guidance as I live a life that is morally pleasing to you. I pray to be a woman of character and virtue. I pray for power to walk in sobriety for you have called us to be sober. I desire to be sober in my thinking which impacts my speaking and actions. I will be alert and watchful that I may resist the enemy and all of his schemes that I may not fall into sin. I will not be a woman who is asleep, careless and unaware, but on the contrary, I will live awake discerning all things. I am not of the night, and therefore I do not live a life engaged in sin and condemnation as those of the night. I pray for solidity through the Holy Spirit to put on the full armor; that I may be covered and protected as I go into the world sharing the light of Christ.

I surrender this prayer in the name of Jesus Christ,

Amen.

#sheslit

Day
28

"

AS THE SUN CAN BE SEEN ONLY BY IT'S OWN LIGHT, SO CHRIST CAN BE **KNOWN** ONLY BY HIS OWN SPIRIT.

— *Robert Leighton*

Day TWENTY EIGHT
See The Good!

TODAY'S SCRIPTURE:
"In the same way, let your good deeds shine out for all to see, so that everyone will praise your heavenly Father."

- Mathew 5:16 (NLT)

PRAYER OF LIGHT:

Dear Father,

I have been privileged by your love and grace to be a recipient of light. And with this light comes a great responsibility that is rooted in love. This responsibility calls for me to share the same light that you have so freely given to me with the world. Each day you bestow upon me the gift of life, I am determined to make a conscious decision to live a life that is honorable and pleasing to you. I choose to live a life that is rooted in light, so that my character is one of integrity. I will use words that are positive, truthful and full of wisdom. I will walk in the light of your love each day which will cause me to constantly crave righteousness and a life of holiness.

My life will speak to your love and the power of forgiveness and your ability to save all who are willing to call upon your name. I desire to live and behave in such a way in which the world will recognize your light in me and glorify you by giving you their lives completely. For it is my character and the volume in which my life will speak that will serve as an example for the world to see and believe.

I surrender this prayer in the name of Jesus Christ,

Amen.

#sheslit

Day

29

" THOUGH THE LIGHT SHINES ON THINGS UNCLEAN, YET IT IS NOT THEREBY DEFILED.

– Augustine

Day TWENTY NINE
Salvation Is Near!

TODAY'S SCRIPTURE:

"This is all the more urgent, for you know how late it is; time is running out. Wake up, for our salvation is nearer now than when we first believed. The night is almost gone; the day of salvation will soon be here. So remove your dark deeds like dirty clothes, and put on the shining armor of right living."

– Romans 13:11-12 (NLT)

PRAYER OF LIGHT:

Dear Father,

As a sober woman of the day, I am alert in the spirit recognizing that you are soon to return to collect those who have kept your commandments and loved your ways. Knowing this, I do not live in the world asleep and uninformed of who you are and how you require me to live as a woman of God. I am not of the night and I deliberately distance myself from those things that do not bring glory and honor to your name. I refuse to accept the works of darkness for I am a woman of light. I pray for toughness and moral force to walk upright and circumspect as I live in a world of darkness.

I pray that your Holy Spirit would rest, rule and abide in my life so that my character will reflect you as I strive to live a life of light. I do not revel in the things of darkness which glorify sin and shame. I reject the things that promote hate, drunkenness, deceit and evil. I commit myself to love, kindness, truth and self-control. By doing this, I display the light of Christ in this dark world.

I surrender this prayer in the name of Jesus Christ,

Amen.

#sheslit

Day
30

"

THE ISSUE IS NOW **CLEAR.** IT IS BETWEEN LIGHT AND DARKNESS AND EVERYONE MUST CHOOSE HIS SIDE.

— *G.K. Chesterton*

Day THIRTY
Evil Exposed!

TODAY'S SCRIPTURE:

"It is shameful even to talk about the things that ungodly people do in secret."

– Ephesians 5:12 (NLT)

PRAYER OF LIGHT:

Dear Father,

We know that whatever is in darkness must be exposed when it comes in contact with light. I pray for courage and boldness to exercise my light in the world as a believer so those who do not believe would see the error of their ways and gladly come into the redeeming light of Christ to be saved and transformed. Give me the fortitude and confidence to live a life of unadulterated love and light. Not as one who judges and condemns, but as a woman who is an example of what can happen when we choose to wake up from sleeping and embrace the light of Christ and all that it brings into our lives.

I pray to be vigilant in sharing the gospel, not only through my words but through my deeds. Give me wisdom, clarity and creativity as I shine in darkness and speak words of light to a dark and sleeping world. While I know that I am empowered and encouraged to share the light that you have bestowed upon me through Christ, I also know that it is you God who draws men and women unto you that they may truly be saved. Awaken their hearts God. Remove the scales from their eyes and cause them to come into your light that they may have life everlasting.

I surrender this prayer in the name of Jesus Christ,

Amen.

#sheslit

Day
31

GIVE LIGHT, AND THE DARKNESS WILL **DISAPPEAR** OF ITSELF.

- Desiderius Erasmus

Day THIRTY ONE
Walk In The Light!

PRAYER OF LIGHT

Dear Father,

I acknowledge you today as the Messiah who is the one and only true light. I live in a world that is steeped in darkness, but you God are the light and you have made your light accessible to those who will follow you. In a society that loves darkness, today I choose the light. I choose to follow you. I choose to lay aside my own will, my own desires and plans and I will follow hard after you and your light. Apart from you there is only darkness and destruction. You are the meaning of life. In you there is clarity and purpose. In you my path is illuminated and my direction is made known. Because I choose you, I choose light. With this choice also comes light.

Today I rejoice in the gift of light that you so freely offer me through your abundant love. Give me strength to follow without intimidation or restriction.

I surrender this prayer in the name of Jesus Christ,

Amen.

#sheslit

Day
32

"

IF I FORGET THAT IT WAS HE WHO GRANTED THAT RAY OF LIGHT TO HIS MOST UNWORTHY SERVANT, THEN I KNOW NOTHING OF CALVARY LOVE.

-Amy Carmichael

Day THIRTY TWO
The Lamp Of The Body!

TODAY'S SCRIPTURE:

"Your eye is like a lamp that provides light for your body. When your eye is healthy, your whole body is filled with light. But when your eye is unhealthy, your whole body is filled with darkness. And if the light you think you have is actually darkness, how deep that darkness is!"
– Mathew 6:22-23 (NLT)

PRAYER OF LIGHT:

Dear Father,

I am grateful for the analogy used in this passage to teach me what is healthy and unhealthy. I understand in your word that through the eye my body receives light and illumination. I am aware that if my eye is good, meaning if my motives are pure and upright, with a desire to live a life that is completely yielded to you, then my life as a result will be flooded with light. This light will impact my entire life and will be displayed through my actions which display kingdom living. However, I am also made aware, that if my eye is bad, then darkness consumes my body for my vision is impaired and I will produce actions of iniquity which go against the kingdom. Today Lord, I pray that my body is good so that my body may be overflowing with light. I am light, for I am a reflection of you.

I surrender this prayer in the name of Jesus Christ,

Amen.

#sheslit

Day
33

"

IF YOU HAVE
ONLY A
LITTLE RAY
OF **LIGHT,**
SHOW OUT
DISTINCTLY
THAT YOU
ARE FOR
HIM.

- G.V. Wigram

Day THIRTY THREE
Living In The Light!

PRAYER OF LIGHT:

Dear Father,

My relationship with others is a direct reflection of my relationship with you. To hate my fellow brother or sister is to embrace the characteristics of darkness. However, to love is to embrace the characteristics of Christ and all that they embody. As your daughter, I am called to love and when I demonstrate anything but love, I am showing the world through my conduct that my heart is far from you and I have not been born again and do not honor the qualities of Christ.

Today I cleanse my heart and distance myself from anything that promotes hate and I freely embrace love as you have so freely loved me. Give me a heart and sensitivity for my brothers and sisters so that I can always show love and walk in your light. As I accept all mankind through love, I do not stumble and I pray that I do not cause others to stumble. As I live in a world that fuels and perpetuates hate, I will be valiant enough to give love and light. I will be love, speak love, see love and share love so that those who encounter me will also encounter your love which is displayed through me.

I surrender this prayer in the name of Jesus Christ,

Amen.

#sheslit

Day
34

" AT TIMES OUR OWN LIGHT GOES OUT AND IS REKINDLED BY A SPARK FROM ANOTHER PERSON.

- Albert Schweitzer

Day THIRTY FOUR
You Are The Light!

TODAY'S SCRIPTURE:
"For the Lord gave us this command when he said, 'I have made you a light to the Gentiles, to bring salvation to the farthest corners of the earth."

- Acts 13:47 (NLT)

PRAYER OF LIGHT:

Dear Father,

In this passage that was taken from Isaiah 49:6, as you spoke to the messiah which was also spoken of by your servants Paul and Barnabas, that as your daughter, you have set me as a light to those who are most in need of you. I will not be intimidated by the world and those who hate the light. I will have valor, live boldly and unafraid through the power of your Holy Spirit as an instrument of light and salvation to all.

This day, I pray that you would use me. That I would be in partnership with the Holy Spirit, humbly yielding myself as a vessel to ensure that every gift, talent and skill be of use to bring light and salvation to a dark and callous world in order to advance your kingdom on the earth. Allow my life, my words and my works to be a living example of your salvation and light in the life of a woman who could never be worthy of your forgiveness and grace. I am grateful for your love towards me and I will show this gratitude by displaying your love to the world and shining your light as I represent you and your kingdom.

I surrender this prayer in the name of Jesus Christ,

Amen.

#sheslit

Day
35

FAITH IS SEEING LIGHT WITH YOUR HEART WHEN ALL YOUR EYES SEE IS DARKNESS.

– Barbara Johnson

Day THIRTY FIVE
You Are Chosen!

TODAY'S SCRIPTURE:

"But you are not like that, for you are a chosen people. You are royal priests, a holy nation, God's very own possession. As a result, you can show others the goodness of God, for he called you out of the darkness into his wonderful light."

- 1 Peter 2:9 (NLT)

PRAYER OF LIGHT:

Dear Father,

When considering this passage, I also consider the promises you made to Israel in Exodus 19:5, to make them "A kingdom of priests and a holy nation" If they would obey you. Through their disobedience, Israel abandoned their place, which the church now occupies. As an heir and joint-heir with you, I understand that I am of a chosen generation, a royal priesthood, a holy nation. I am distinct and I have been designated to proclaim your praises. I was created to declare your love. It was you and only you who called me out of sin and darkness into your magnificent light. It was you who looked upon me with love and sent your only begotten son to die, to take my place on the cross that I might be saved and delivered from condemnation.

My heart is appreciative and my spirit rejoices that you are my God. I will forever proclaim your praises for your loving kindness and tender mercies toward me. Thank you for choosing me. I pray to become a daily physical expression of your love to the world, so that other women would be drawn to your light and choose to be saved.

I surrender this prayer in the name of Jesus Christ,

Amen.

#sheslit

Day
36

"

BE BOLD AND **FEARLESS** IN SHINNING YOUR LIGHT! THE WORLD NEEDS IT!

- Karri Turner, M.Div.

Day THIRTY SIX
Equally Yoked!

PRAYER OF LIGHT:

Dear Father,

As I consider this text, I also consider Deuteronomy 22:10 where clean and unclean animals were not to be yoked together. Paul also shares that as a believer, we are not to connect ourselves with those who are spiritually of a different nature. I was created to bring you glory and this is impossible to do when I yoke myself closely with those who do not believe in you.

I pray for power today to separate myself from any relationship that is not equivalent in the spirit. I will not connect myself to people or situations that produce disobedience, iniquity, darkness and the desire to promote idolatry. I declare that every personal, romantic and business relationship will be one that is founded on belief in you and will not compromise the integrity of my faith and testimony. I will live a life that is governed by your word, of which I will hide in my heart to produce moral behavior that will be an example of light in a dark world. My entire existence is to please you and bring glory and honor to your name.

I surrender this prayer in the name of Jesus Christ,

Amen.

#sheslit

Day
37

"

ALWAYS BE MINDFUL THAT YOU ARE A VESSEL OF LIGHT OR OF DARKNESS! WHICH WILL YOU BE?

- Karri Turner, M.Div.

Day THIRTY SEVEN
You Cannot Disguise The Light!

TODAY'S SCRIPTURE:

"These people are false apostles. They are deceitful workers who disguise themselves as apostles of Christ."

-2 Corinthians 11:13 (NLT)

PRAYER OF LIGHT:

Dear Father,

Each day I come face-to-face with evil as it presents itself to me based upon some of my deepest hopes and longings. Evil knows some of the most intimate parts of who I am and uses those very desires to try to manipulate, abuse and seduce me, to draw me out of your will into a life of darkness. Evil is not presented as it is, but it comes as an illusion of what is good. Evil presents itself as false apostles, leaders, preachers and teachers who do not follow your ways within their hearts, but give the outward appearance of representing you. They display an outward appearance of righteousness; however, their hearts are far from you. They proclaim a word contrary to who you are. They are representatives of Satan, who are not transformed by the Word of God, but are instruments yielded to darkness.

I pray today for your covering and protection. I pray for increased discernment that I may "try the spirit, by the spirit," to know who is truly of you and who is not. I pray for strength to see in the spirit, that I will not be overtaken by the deceiver and his tactics. I declare that I am fortified in your word and powered by your Holy Spirit.

I surrender this prayer in the name of Jesus Christ,

Amen.

#sheslit

Day
38

" WORDS WHICH DO NOT GIVE THE LIGHT OF CHRIST INCREASE THE DARKNESS.

- Mother Theresa

Day THIRTY EIGHT
Works That Glorify God!

TODAY'S SCRIPTURE:
"In the same way, let your good deeds shine out for all to see, so that everyone will praise your heavenly Father."
- Mathew 5:14-15 (NLT)

PRAYER OF LIGHT:

Dear Father,

Just as Jesus Christ is the "light of the world," as a woman who confesses to be a believer, a Christian, I am also called to be the "light of the world." Jesus is my source and I will be unashamed as I reflect this in a dark and dreary world. I will not try to hide or dim my light in effort to fit in with the world or accommodate those who do not love or understand you. I will not shrink back or become intimidated by darkness, but I will go forth as light, exposing those things that are not of you and declaring your truth. I will be the light in my home, on my job, in my school, in my business, at my church and in all of my relationships and daily encounters with people from all sectors of life. I realize that I have been elevated, not to boast or for self-promotion, but to shine brightly for all to see. To bring light in the midst of darkness as a living example of your light and love. I will not surpress my light, but only do as you have required, which is to shine my light on all those who I encounter near and far.

I surrender this prayer in the name of Jesus Christ,

Amen.

#sheslit

Day
39

"

THE LIGHT
OF CHRIST
ILLUMINES
ALL.

– Gregory Palamas

Day THIRTY NINE
The Light Of The Lord!

PRAYER OF LIGHT:

Dear Father,

You are the source of all that is good. You are incorruptible and completely perfect. You do not just "do good," but you are the embodiment of good. Light springs forth from you. You created the sun, moon and stars for us to physically experience light while on earth, yet you are also the spiritual light that leads the way. While the world is fickle, ever-changing, shifting, evolving and adjusting, based on a variety of unstable variables, you remain unmoved and unchanged. As humans we change day-by-day depending upon the circumstance or situation. We are often governed by our feelings and emotions which can lead us down paths of unrighteousness. However, you do not change, and there is no shadow of turning in you. You are a fortified and unmovable force. There is no variableness in you. Your love and consistency are unmatched.

Your gifts are as good and as perfect as you are. You do not draw or tempt us to sin, but temptation comes from our own lusts and sinful nature. Your gifts personify your love and grace towards us. They are everything divine causing us to lack for nothing.

I surrender this prayer in the name of Jesus Christ,

Amen.

#sheslit

Day
40

"

DO NOT GO GENTLE INTO THAT GOOD NIGHT BUT RAGE, RAGE AGAINST THE DYING OF THE LIGHT.

— Dylan Thomas

Day FOURTY
I Will Rise!

TODAY'S SCRIPTURE:

*"Do not gloat over me, my enemies!
For though I fall, I will rise again.
Though I sit in darkness, the Lord will
be my light."*

- Psalm 89:15 (NLT)

PRAYER OF LIGHT:

Dear Father,

Today I boldly warn my enemy and the workers of darkness that it is in you that I trust. Even in times of rebuke and chastisement I will trust in you. I repent of my sin and realize that all sin must be punished. Yet with humility and patience, I will wait for you during my affliction. For my difficulty is due to the sin in which I have brought upon myself. During this time of difficulty, I am encouraged for I trust that you will never leave nor forsake me. I rest in the fact that your love is unfailing and your anger is yet but a moment. Through faith I look to you, for you are my hope and salvation!

Therefore, I can confidently declare to my enemies not to rejoice over me when I fall for it will not be long before you lift me up and cause me to rise again. While I may be experiencing hardship and suffering in my time of darkness, you God have not abandoned me. You are my light and my hope. I am strengthened to recover and to recover well!

I surrender this prayer in the name of Jesus Christ,

Amen.

#sheslit

GO FORTH *Lit*

Stay In Touch!

@mzkarribaby

@karriturner

@thekarriturner

WWW.KARRITURNER.ORG

Made in the USA
San Bernardino, CA
24 July 2018